# SLEEPLESS IN SANGRIA

## 60 ROMCOM COCKTAILS YOU'LL FALL IN LOVE WITH

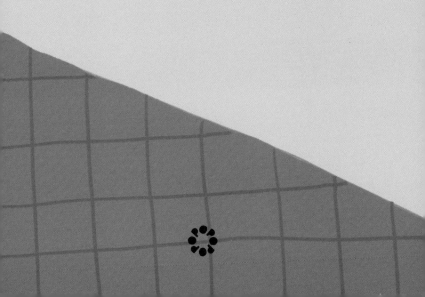

# CONTENTS

# IT'S ALL ABOUT THE CHEMISTRY

What is it that makes a perfect romantic comedy? And, while we are here, what about the perfect cocktail? Could they have something in common?

It shouldn't be too sweet or cloying. But neither do we want something too sour or challenging – we are here to enjoy ourselves after all! Perhaps it's about finding the perfect balance then, about all the ingredients coming together to create something that's just a little bit magic.

It's hard to explain why some cocktails have stood the test of time and are still being made and enjoyed even a hundred years after they were first concocted, in places like Harry's Bar in Venice (the Bellini), Raffles Hotel's Long Bar in Singapore (the Singapore Sling) or the Manhattan Club in New York (the Manhattan). Maybe we shouldn't try, then – just like we don't need to understand exactly what it is that makes us take Bridget Jones, Sally Albright or Cher Horowitz into our hearts and cheer them on as they navigate life, love and relationships. We just do.

Sure, some people may *claim* they don't like romcoms but, just like cocktails, there is one out there for everyone. Whether you get swept up in the romance of *Sleepless in Seattle*, fall for the classic charms of *Breakfast at Tiffany's* or laugh out loud at the pratfalls of the *Wedding Crashers*, as the movies themselves show us again and again, you have to be open to possibilities if you are going to find your perfect match.

And that is what this book is here to do! In these pages, you will find recipes for 60 cocktails inspired by our favourite romcoms, designed to bring all their charm straight to your glass. Some you will recognise, some you won't, but you are guaranteed to have a good time while you get to know them. And remember, sometimes the drink of your dreams might have been there all along, waiting for you to notice it, and other times, it might suddenly arrive in your life and change everything. Either way, *Sleepless in Sangria* is here to play matchmaker, making that all-important meet-cute happen.

The traditional romantic comedy story is all about bringing the couple together – though they first have to navigate a few obstacles, of course. But the films are about connections for their viewers too. Is there anything cosier than sitting on the sofa with people you care about and putting on a movie you have loved your whole life, or something you have been meaning to see, and laughing (and maybe crying!) at it together? It could be a date, a group of friends, your BFF or even your parents – introducing them to one of your favourites or watching something they first enjoyed when they were your age. And what better way to celebrate that connection than by making a cocktail to settle down with first?

Whatever you like in a leading lady or leading man – whether you prefer the sass of Reese Witherspoon or the bubbliness of Drew Barrymore; the rugged good looks of Ryan Reynolds or the understated charm of Henry Golding – you will find it all on screen. No date can be so awkward, no working day so dull, no Sunday afternoon so rainy that a romcom can't make you feel better.

So, let's raise a glass of whatever cocktail takes your fancy to the magic of romcoms and make a toast: here's to finding the cheese to your macaroni.

All the cocktails in this recipe book are made for a single serving and you can multiply up depending on how many you're serving. Glasses are also suggestions, so don't let a lack of specific glassware stop you from having fun! And if you would be interested in making your own sugar syrup, here's an easy guide.

## HOW TO MAKE YOUR OWN SUGAR SYRUP

Essentially this is just sugar and water and all the recipes in this book require a mix in the ratio of 1:1 by volume. However, if you do see the use of 2:1 for other recipes, that simply refers to the use of double the sugar to the water. You can make these easily at home and create a batch so you have it to hand when you fancy a drink.

A 1:1 mix is possible using a blender; just add equal volumes of water and sugar to a blender and blend until well mixed.

To make a 2:1 syrup you will generally need heat to ensure the sugar dissolves in the water. Heat the water gently in a pan, add half of the sugar. Stir briefly and leave until the mixture becomes clear. Add the remaining sugar and repeat. Be careful not to over-stir; the mixture will clarify on its own if left, without agitation.

# THE RECIPES

# I'LL HAVE WHAT SHE'S HAVING

Can rum and lime juice ever be friends? When you add a soupçon of sugar syrup, then yes, they can! In fact, these ingredients bring a lightness and bite worthy of a script by the high priestess of romcoms, Nora Ephron herself. Show your appreciation as loudly as you like.

# WHEN HARRY MET DAIQUIRI

## INGREDIENTS

50ML WHITE RUM          20ML LIME JUICE          15ML SUGAR SYRUP (SEE PAGE 9)

Add all the ingredients to a cocktail shaker with a good amount of ice. As we know, nothing exciting happens unless you shake things up, so really make sure these ingredients are combined! Double-strain into a chilled martini glass or champagne coupe. Classically, the daiquiri is garnished with a lime wedge on the rim of the glass, but hey, who said you had to stick to the rules...

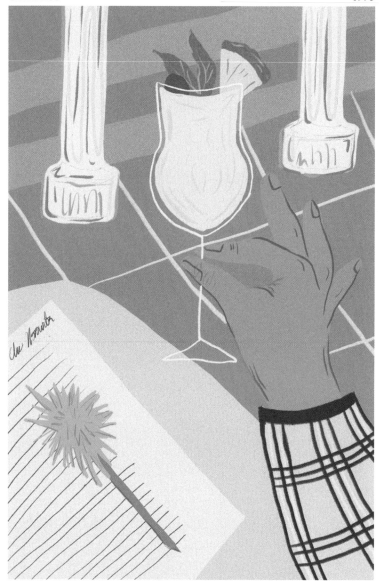

A cocktail that's a little bit extra, but sweet and adorable at the same time, just like everyone's favourite yellow plaid-wearing heroine, Cher Horowitz. Go wild on your garnishes – from pineapple slices and cherries to umbrellas and bright pink paper straws – to make sure your drink is a total Baldwin, and never a Monet.

# CLUELESS COLADA

## INGREDIENTS

50ML WHITE RUM

50ML COCONUT CREAM

150ML PINEAPPLE JUICE (OR FRESH PINEAPPLE, BLENDED TO JUICE)

Add all the ingredients to a cocktail shaker with ice and shake well. Strain into a tall glass filled with ice. And don't forget to have fun with those garnishes!

Flavourful, botanical gin and zesty lime – they might have competing agendas, but when two ingredients are this evenly matched, sparks are going to fly! Resist it all you want, but no one was ever bored by the perfect gimlet. Just think carefully before hopping on the back of a strange man's motorbike while wearing a backless dress.

# HOW TO LOSE A GIMLET IN 10 DAYS

## INGREDIENTS

50ML NAVY-STRENGTH GIN
(I.E., 57 PER CENT ABV OR MORE)

50ML LIME JUICE CORDIAL

Rose's lime juice cordial is the classic here, but you could also make your own from lime juice and zest, water, sugar and citric acid. Add both ingredients to a mixing glass and stir. Strain into a chilled martini glass or champagne coupe.

This might not be the most elegant of drinks (no one is going to accuse it of having been photoshopped, let's be honest) and it might seem like, well, a bit of a bro. But, just like Jacob Palmer, it has hidden depths. The perfect light and refreshing drink, it deserves to be given a chance.

# CRAZY SHANDY LOVE

## INGREDIENTS

| 275ML BEER | 275ML LEMONADE | SLICE OF LEMON |
|---|---|---|

Put the slice of lemon onto the rim of a tall or pint glass. Then, whilst holding your glass at a 45-degree angle, pour in the lemonade and beer. Easy as doing a handstand push-up (if you're Ryan Gosling...).

Kat may have had a point that you don't need to do something just because everyone else is doing it, but that doesn't mean you should resist giving this cocktail a go. Not quite as good as being serenaded by Heath Ledger, backed by a full marching band, but close.

# 10 THINGS I HATE ABOUT WOO WOO

## INGREDIENTS

25ML PEACH SCHNAPPS
50ML VODKA

120ML CRANBERRY JUICE
JUICE OF ¼ LIME

LIME WEDGE (TO GARNISH)

Add the peach schnapps, vodka, cranberry juice and lime juice to a cocktail shaker filled with ice. Shake and strain into a tall tumbler half-filled with ice. Garnish with a lime wedge.

Maybe there is a bossy ghost in your apartment, maybe you just have an annoying housemate. Either way, forget work for a while and try this punchy cocktail that's based on a drink originally designed to wake the dead – or, well, the quite hungover. It's what Reese Witherspoon would have wanted.

# *The Tenant Reviver*

## INGREDIENTS

| | | |
|---|---|---|
| 25ML GIN | 25ML LILLET BLANC VERMOUTH | 2–3 DASHES ABSINTHE |
| 25ML TRIPLE SEC | 25ML LEMON JUICE | LEMON, TO GARNISH |

Add all the ingredients to a cocktail shaker with ice and shake well. Strain into a large gin bowl or champagne coupe. Garnish with a twist of lemon zest.

If you've never tried this boozy, champagne-fuelled cocktail, then it's time to lose your V-card. And if people talk – well, let them. Romcom heroes and heroines don't listen to gossip and that's why they get to ride off into the sunset with the person of their choosing at the end. In this case, on a lawnmower.

# EASY (A)MBROSIA

## INGREDIENTS

| | | |
|---|---|---|
| 25ML COGNAC | 1 TSP TRIPLE SEC | CHAMPAGNE |
| 25ML CALVADOS | 1 TSP LEMON JUICE | |

Pour all the ingredients (except for the champagne) into a cocktail shaker. Add ice and shake well. Strain into a champagne flute or champagne coupe, then top up with champagne exactly to your liking and serve immediately.

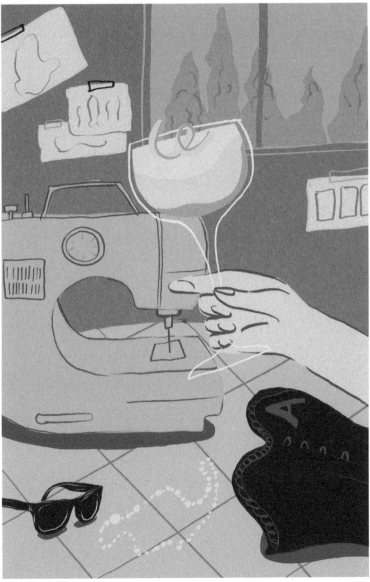

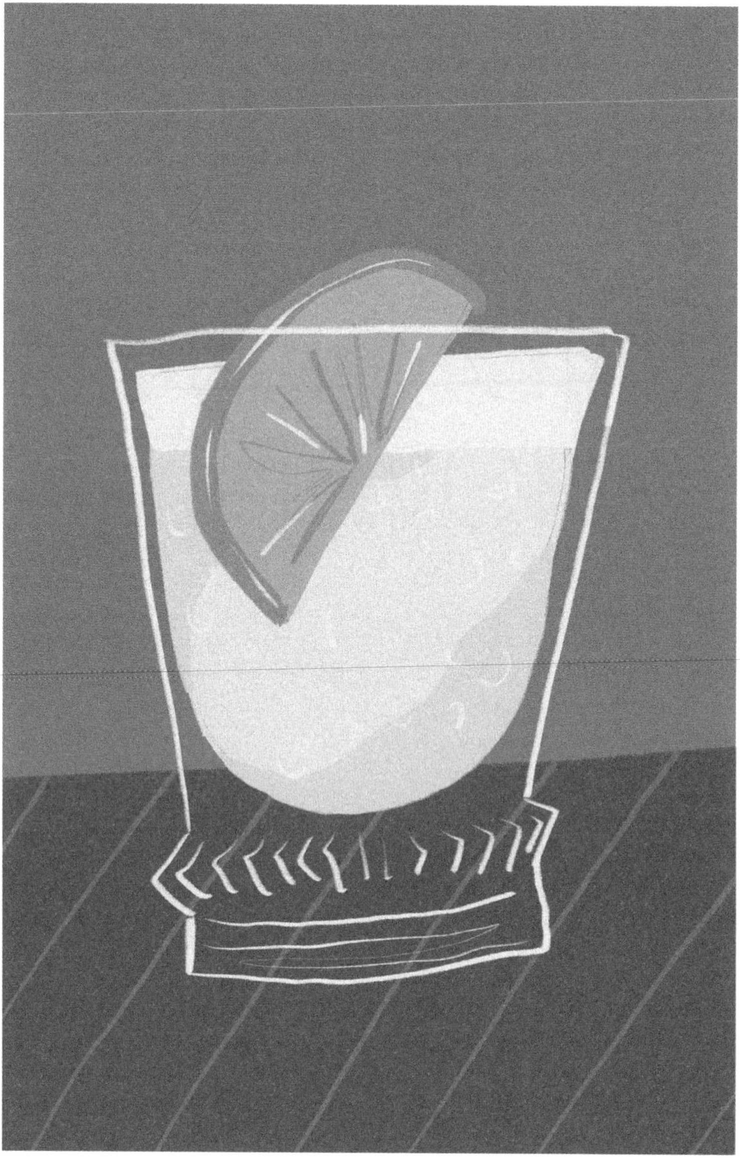

*What?* You might be thinking. *Whisky, absinthe, egg white, lemon AND lime?* Well, sometimes you just can't predict who or what you are going to be attracted to. It might be what is essentially a grown-up Southern Comfort and lemonade, it might be a chauvinistic Gerard Butler. Just try to avoid a super-awkward snog in a lift.

# MORNING SHOW FIZZ

## INGREDIENTS

50ML SCOTCH WHISKY

25ML LEMON/LIME JUICE MIX (50:50)

15ML SUGAR SYRUP (SEE PAGE 9)

EGG WHITE

1–2 DASHES ABSINTHE

SODA WATER

ORANGE, TO GARNISH

Add all the ingredients (except the soda water) to a cocktail shaker. Shake without ice to emulsify the egg white. Add ice and shake again. Strain into a tall tumbler (no ice) and top up with soda water. Finish with a slice of orange.

Warning: this cocktail packs a punch, so go easy, particularly in times of emotional turmoil, like if you find out your dad is dating your ex. Drink too many of these and the ending will be somewhat predictable... It's a good drink though, so try it once, and if you want to commit,  well, that's up to you!

# No Strings Between the Sheets

## INGREDIENTS

| | | |
|---|---|---|
| 20ML WHITE RUM | 20ML COINTREAU | LIME, TO GARNISH |
| 20ML COGNAC | 10ML LEMON JUICE | |

Add all the ingredients to a cocktail shaker, along with ice, and shake well.
Strain into a chilled round glass or champagne coupe. Garnish with a lime twist.

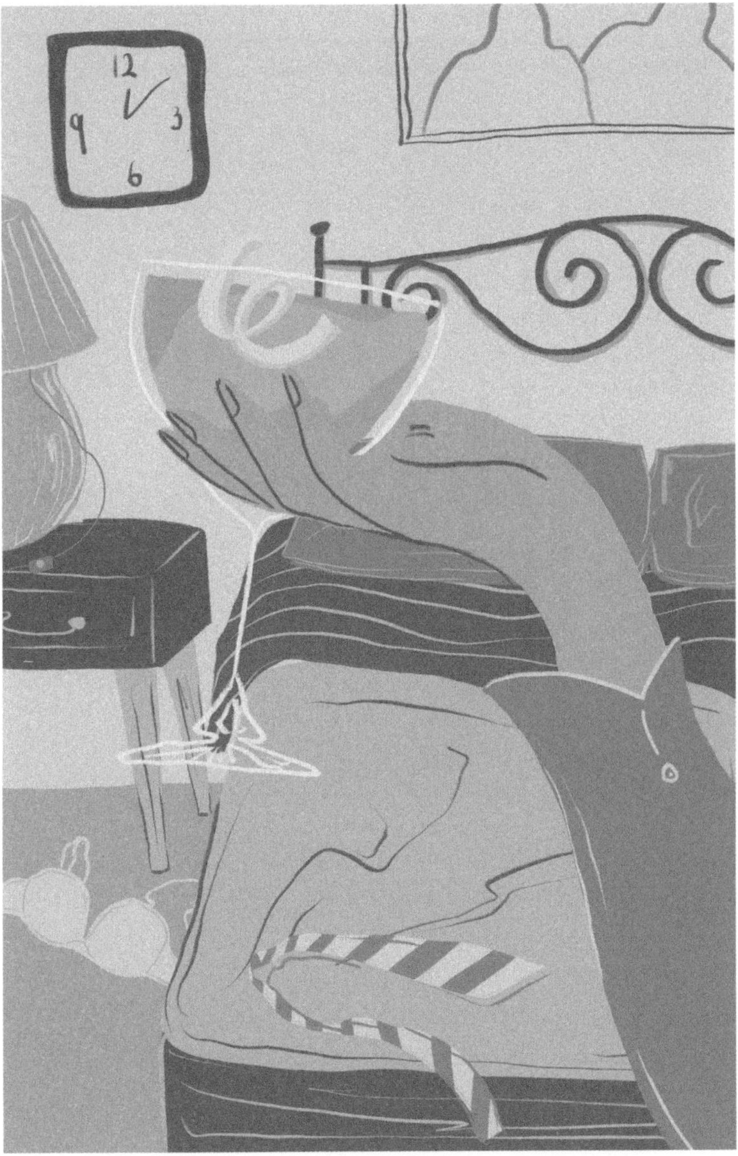
12
9
3
6

What would you do differently knowing what you know now? That's a pretty profound question and, realistically, one probably best tackled after a cocktail. We all dreamed of being popular and grown-up when we were 13, but adulthood isn't all Manhattan apartments and cool jobs on magazines. Never mind – good friends, cocktails and romcoms is a pretty good deal, even without access to magic dust.

# Matty-dor

## INGREDIENTS

| | | |
|---|---|---|
| 30ML BLANCO TEQUILA | 60ML PINEAPPLE JUICE | SOME FRUIT, TO GARNISH |
| 20ML LIME JUICE | | |

Add all the ingredients to a cocktail shaker. Shake hard over ice to ensure that the pineapple juice is well mixed (until it's a smooth texture and a foam develops on top). Strain into a chilled round glass or champagne coupe. Garnish with a slice of fruit, like a lime slice or pineapple wedge.

Ah! A pre-McConaughey-sance romcom classic, from back in the days when he was happy to play charming bad boys with a good heart. Don't get stuck drinking the same thing because it's comfortable and easy – try this zippy cocktail with a kick. Just like SJP and McConaughey, lime and tequila really do have the perfect chemistry.

# *Tripp Sour*

## INGREDIENTS

| | | |
|---|---|---|
| 50ML TEQUILA | 20ML SUGAR SYRUP (SEE PAGE 9) | FRUIT, TO GARNISH |
| 25ML LIME JUICE | EGG WHITE OR 2 TBSP WHIPPED AQUAFABA | |

Add all the ingredients to a cocktail shaker. Shake without ice, then add ice and shake again. Strain into a short rumbler/rocks glass over ice. Garnish with a slice of apple and a cherry or two.

Underestimate this cocktail at your peril. Sure, it might look kind-of pink and frivolous but, as Elle Woods is here to teach us, appearances can be deceptive – this is actually a classic Cuban cocktail that goes back to Prohibition era. You could make a strong case that it is even better than spending four hours in a hot tub after winter formal.

# ELLE SORORITY PRESIDENTE

## INGREDIENTS

| | | |
|---|---|---|
| 60ML RUM | 10ML CURAÇAO OR TRIPLE SEC | ORANGE, TO GARNISH |
| 30ML DRY VERMOUTH | 1 DASH GRENADINE | |

Fill a mixing glass with ice. Add all the ingredients and stir until chilled. Strain into a chilled martini glass or short tumbler and garnish with an orange wedge. Then the prosecution may rest.

Whether you loved high school, like Rob, or it was a traumatic time of not quite fitting in, like Josie, let it all go and make yourself this classic cocktail, while wondering if South Glen High shouldn't perhaps have had some security measures in place to stop adult reporters spying on their students...

# JOSIE'S JULEP

## INGREDIENTS

A COUPLE OF SPRIGS OF MINT          60ML BOURBON          20ML SUGAR SYRUP (SEE PAGE 9)

Add all of the ingredients to a short tumbler or julep cup and stir gently. Leave for 10 minutes or so for the mint to infuse. Add crushed ice and churn with a spoon (preferably a bar spoon as the metal disc on one end is perfect for pulling the mint up through the ice). Top up with more ice and churn again. Garnish with a mint sprig or two. If you want to be super-profesh, slap the mint against your hand a couple of times first to bring out the mint oils.

# SUMMER OF LOVE

A drink that you just won't be able to stop thinking about and perfect for a beach holiday – whether or not you run into your ex there. As the wisdom of Kunu might have it, if life hands you limes, you've at least got one of the ingredients for a great mai tai.

# FORGETTING SARAH MAI TAI

## INGREDIENTS

30ML JAMAICAN RUM
30ML AGRICOLE RUM
30ML LIME JUICE

15ML CURAÇAO
10ML ORGEAT SYRUP

10ML SUGAR SYRUP (SEE PAGE 9)
FRUIT, TO GARNISH

Add all the ingredients to a cocktail shaker, along with some crushed or cracked ice, and shake well. Strain into short tumbler filled with ice and garnish with a pineapple chunk, cherries, a mint spring, and an umbrella if you have one to hand.

Before Tom met Meg, there was Daryl Hannah, a beautiful mermaid, with hair we were all obsessed with, when we were seven. A sweeter, lighter version of a martini, this is a perfect New York drink that Madison would surely approve of. You can drink it in the bath if you like, but in that case, maybe just limit it to one!

# TOM HANKY PANKY

## INGREDIENTS

| | | |
|---|---|---|
| 30ML SWEET VERMOUTH | 2 DASHES FERNET-BRANCA | ORANGE, TO GARNISH |
| 30ML GIN | | |

Put all the ingredients into a mixing glass with ice. Stir and strain into a martini glass or champagne coupe – chilled if possible, you want this colder than the Hudson River – and garnish with a neatly twisted strip of orange zest.

# TOP 3
# TOM HANK
# ROMCOMS

**1**
## *SLEEPLESS IN SEATTLE*
**(1993)**

**2**
## *YOU'VE GOT MAIL*
**(1998)**

**3**
## *SPLASH*
**(1984)**

Whether your life is currently one big musical number, or your boss has decided you are fit only to write condolence cards, a chilled and herby mojito could be just what you need. It's perfect if you are a little tired of sweet, fruity cocktails and you're looking for a different perspective.

# 500 FLAVOURS OF MOJITO

## INGREDIENTS

| | | |
|---|---|---|
| 20ML LIME JUICE | COUPLE OF SPRIGS OF MINT | SODA WATER |
| 15ML SUGAR SYRUP (SEE PAGE 9) | 50ML WHITE RUM | |

Add the lime juice, sugar syrup and mint leaves to a tall tumbler. Lightly muddle the mixture. Add the rum and half-fill the glass with ice. Stir well with a bar spoon and top with more ice to fill the glass, then add a splash of soda water to taste. Garnish with a couple of mint leaves. The amount of ice in this drink makes it much easier to drink with a straw! Sip thoughtfully while contemplating architecture.

Much like Melanie Smooter/Carmichael, this is a cocktail that seems to be made up of parts that don't quite fit together – American whiskey and the English classic sloe gin? Whaaaat? But shake it all up and somehow it works. Sure, other drinks might have the refinement of a proposal in Tiffany's, but where's the fun in that?

# SWEET HOME ALABAMA SLAMMER

## INGREDIENTS

25ML SOUTHERN COMFORT (OR SIMILAR AMERICAN WHISKEY)

25ML SLOE GIN

25ML AMARETTO

50ML ORANGE JUICE (FRESHLY SQUEEZED IS BEST)

ORANGE AND CHERRY, TO GARNISH

Add all the spirits to a cocktail shaker along with the orange juice and ice. Shake well and strain into a small tumbler or martini glass over ice. Garnish with a wedge of orange or a cherry.

It's the classic drink that everyone wants. But there's no need to fight over it, and you won't have to hire a private investigator to find it, as the recipe is right here! It's perfect for a lazy late brunch or a Sunday pick-me-up and, while no one is about to claim that cocktails are good for you, a good dose of tomato juice is certainly a heartening addition.

# There's Something About (Bloody) Mary

## INGREDIENTS

50ML VODKA

100ML TOMATO JUICE

TABASCO SAUCE (4–10 DROPS, DEPENDING ON HOW HOT YOU WANT THINGS TO GET)

WORCESTERSHIRE SAUCE (2–5 DROPS)

A SPLASH OF LEMON JUICE

BLACK PEPPER (1–2 TWISTS OF A PEPPER GRINDER)

A PINCH OF SALT (CELERY SALT WORKS WELL IF YOU HAVE IT)

CELERY, OLIVES, LEMON AND PICKLES, TO GARNISH

Add all the ingredients to a cocktail shaker, but go slowly with the tabasco and Worcestershire sauces, so you get the kick just how you like it. You might want to play around with the quantity of lemon juice too. Add ice and roll the cocktail shaker, turning it over slowly to allow the ingredients to mix and chill – don't go nuts and shake it as you'll make the drink too watery. Strain into a chilled highball glass, with or without ice. A celery stick is the classic garnish but you can be more inventive if you like!

It's not clear why only boys get to travel through time, but in romcom cocktail land, everyone can change their future – for one, by learning to make this classic rum cocktail! It's definitely something you'll want to revisit, and the perfect accompaniment to a game of ping pong with Bill Nighy.

# BACK IN TIME

## INGREDIENTS

| 10ML SUGAR SYRUP (SEE PAGE 9) | 50ML GOLDEN OR DARK RUM | AN ORANGE |
| --- | --- | --- |
| 2–3 DASHES ANGOSTURA BITTERS | | |

Add a large disc of orange zest to the bottom of a rocks glass along with the sugar syrup, bitters and 25ml of the rum. Add two cubes of ice and stir for 20 to 30 seconds to dilute. Add the remaining rum, two more ice cubes and stir again.

What is there not to love about this cocktail? It's fun, it's silly, it's sweet and it couldn't be easier. Whether you are in Greece trying to untangle some potentially complicated family dynamics, or at home on the sofa on a rainy Saturday, let's sing it together: Cuba libre – how can we resist you?!

# MAMMA
# CUBA LIBRE

## INGREDIENTS

| 2–3 LIME WEDGES | 50ML RUM | 70–100ML COLA |
|---|---|---|

Fill a tumbler with ice. Squeeze in the lime wedges, add the rum and top up with cola. Add more ice to fill the glass (more ice means it won't melt so fast and dilute your drink) or more cola if you need to, but be careful not to overdilute the rum.

Wouldn't it be nice to take a drive out to the Hawaiian countryside to pick a fresh pineapple? (Without the amnesia-causing accident, obviously.) If that's not an option where you live, you can make every day special by trying this boozy, but delightfully tropical cocktail, and settling down to watch the romcom with more meet-cutes than any other.

# OOPSY (BRANDY) DAISY

## INGREDIENTS

50ML COGNAC
10ML TRIPLE SEC OR CURAÇAO
20ML LEMON JUICE

1 TSP SUGAR SYRUP (SEE PAGE 9)
SODA WATER
2 DASHES JAMAICAN RUM

A SPRIG OF MINT AND FRUIT OF YOUR CHOICE FOR A GARNISH – YES, YOU CAN USE FRESH PINEAPPLE!

Add the cognac, triple sec/curaçao, lemon juice and sugar syrup to a cocktail shaker, and fill it up with ice. Shake well and strain into a large wine glass or julep cup filled with ice. Add a splash of soda water and finish with a couple of dashes of Jamaican rum over the top. Garnish with fruits – redcurrants and blackberries look good if you don't go for the pineapple – and a sprig of mint for freshness. Watch out for penguins on the road.

Maybe they'll call you, maybe they won't. Maybe they like you, maybe they don't. If they're not putting the effort in, then they're not the one for you. They're no Bradley Cooper/Jennifer Aniston anyway. This fun, flirty cocktail is the perfect solution to any uninspiring date.

# HE'S JUST NOT THAT INTO SEX ON THE BEACH

## INGREDIENTS

50ML VODKA
25ML PEACH SCHNAPPS
25ML CRÈME DE CASSIS (OPTIONAL)

60ML CRANBERRY JUICE
60ML FRESHLY SQUEEZED ORANGE JUICE

ORANGE AND CHERRY, TO GARNISH

Pour the vodka, peach schnapps and crème de cassis (for a little extra fruitiness if you fancy it) into a highball glass filled two-thirds with ice. Add the cranberry juice and stir to combine. Slowly pour over the freshly squeezed orange juice. Garnish with an orange wedge and cherry.

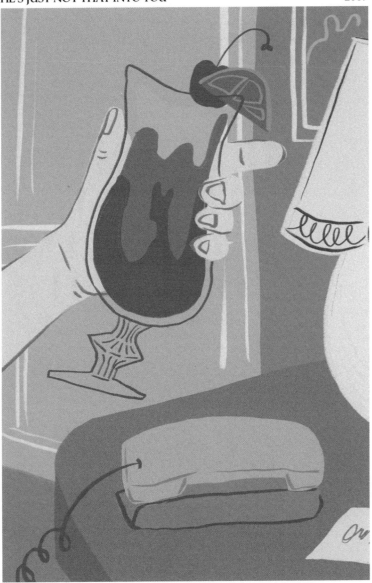

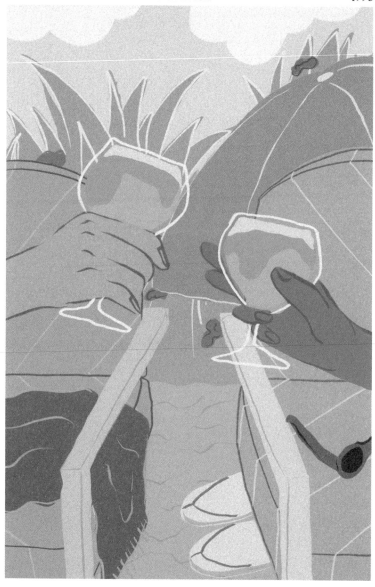

In a decade when romcoms tended to feature blonde ladies dating older men, we needed Stella Payne to come, and shake things up, even more than she needed that holiday in Jamaica. So whip up this punch and pretend you're in an island paradise, about to meet your very own sexy chef.

# STELLA'S GINGER BREW

## INGREDIENTS

40ML GIN

50ML LEMON JUICE

50ML GINGER SYRUP

1 SMALL BOTTLE OF BEER (ALE)

Add the gin, lemon juice and ginger syrup to a blender with a couple of ice cubes. Blend. Fine-strain the mixture into a chilled round glass. Top up with beer.

Were eggs from Juli Baker's chickens ever used to make a rum flip? It feels unlikely, but don't let that stop you, as this old-school cocktail comes with a heavy dose of nostalgia – just like the film itself. Even if it doesn't seem that appealing to begin with, you'll fall for its charms in the end.

# RUM FLIPPED

## INGREDIENTS

| | | |
|---|---|---|
| 50ML RUM | 1 EGG | WHOLE NUTMEG |
| 25ML SUGAR SYRUP (SEE PAGE 9) | | |

Add the rum and sugar syrup to a cocktail shaker. Crack the egg directly in. Shake without ice (dry shake) then add ice and shake again (wet shake). Strain into a chilled large wine glass or champagne coupe and garnish with freshly grated nutmeg.

When Princess Ann, played by Audrey Hepburn, becomes burnt out by too many royal duties, her doctor recommends that she take a break and do whatever she wants for a while. Who can argue with that? This classic American drink is guaranteed to sweep you up in the romance of Hollywood – even if it can't promise Gregory Peck will turn up on his Vespa.

# Ro-Manhattan Holiday

## INGREDIENTS

60ML AMERICAN WHISKEY – BOURBON OR RYE

20ML VERMOUTH (DRY, SWEET OR A 50:50 MIXTURE OF BOTH, DEPENDING ON HOW YOU LIKE IT!)

2–3 DASHES BITTERS

MARASCHINO CHERRY AND LEMON, TO GARNISH (OPTIONAL)

Fill a mixing glass with ice. Add all of the ingredients and stir until chilled. Strain into a chilled glass. This works by itself but if you'd like, you can garnish with a maraschino cherry if you prefer it sweet or perfect, or a strip of lemon zest for those who want it dry.

# DOWN-TOWN DRINKS

No promises, but a chance encounter with this drink just might change your life. Whether you live in Notting Hill or Beverly Hills, or somewhere completely different, this is a cocktail to bring people together. Just be careful that, after a few, you don't decide to climb into any private gardens. Whoopsidaisies.

# NOTTING BELLINI

## INGREDIENTS

1 BOTTLE PROSECCO          4 RIPE WHITE PEACHES

Peel and stone your peaches and blend the fruit in a food processor or with a stick blender until smooth. Refrigerate your peach purée for at least 20 minutes (or until chilled). Either in a jug or in individual champagne flutes, combine one part peach purée with two parts prosecco. Stir to combine.

# ROMCOM KINGS
## HOLLYWOOD'S HIGHEST-GROSSING ROMCOM ACTORS

### 1
# HUGH GRANT

### 2
# RICHARD GERE

### 3
# BEN STILLER

(SOURCE: THE NUMBERS)

'Kiki! Kiki! Make me an Americano Sweetheart!' Whether you have your own personal assistant to rustle up your cocktails for you or not, this is well worth trying. It may not be as famous as its boozy big sister, the Negroni, but it has an understated charm that shouldn't be overlooked. That cocktail you saw by the pool? It was this one!

# Americano Sweethearts

## INGREDIENTS

50ML CAMPARI
50ML SWEET VERMOUTH

SODA WATER

ORANGE, TO GARNISH

Fill a tall glass with ice. Add the Campari and sweet vermouth. Top with soda water to your taste, stir to mix and garnish with a wedge of orange.

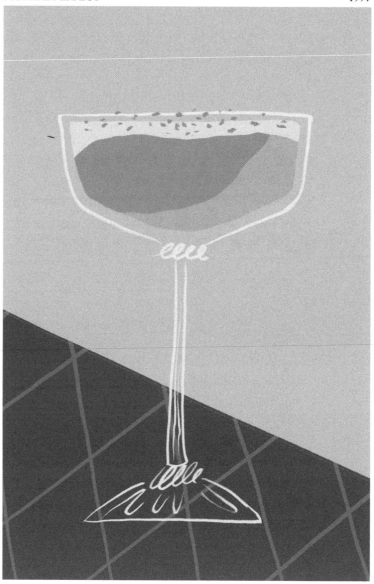

Jennifer Aniston's Kate Mosley clearly did not get the memo from *The Wedding Date's* Kat about what inevitably happens when you pay a guy to pretend to be your fiancé. But we can forgive that (though we may raise an eyebrow at a boss who sees an engagement as a prerequisite for promoting someone) as this film, just like this cocktail, has a certain sweet, old-fashioned charm that is hard to resist.

# BOSTON BOUND

## INGREDIENTS

50ML BOURBON

50ML MADEIRA

10ML SUGAR SYRUP (SEE PAGE 9)

1 EGG

WHOLE NUTMEG

Add the alcohol and sugar syrup to a cocktail shaker, then crack in the egg. Shake without ice, then add ice and shake again. Strain into a chilled martini glass or champagne coupe and garnish with a light sprinkle of freshly grated nutmeg.

Maybe you tried to make this cocktail before and it didn't go so well. Perhaps you ended up with a murky pink mess rather than the sunrise of your dreams. But now you have this recipe, would you do it all over again? Of course you would! See you in Montauk.

# Eternal Tequila Sunrise of the Spotless Mind

## INGREDIENTS

50ML TEQUILA
75ML ORANGE JUICE

1 TBSP GRENADINE

ORANGE, TO GARNISH

Add the tequila and orange juice to a cocktail shaker. Fill with ice and shake. Strain into a tall tumbler glass filled with ice. Gently pour the grenadine down the side of the glass; it is a dense, sticky syrup and will sink to the bottom, creating the sunrise effect. Garnish with an orange wedge.

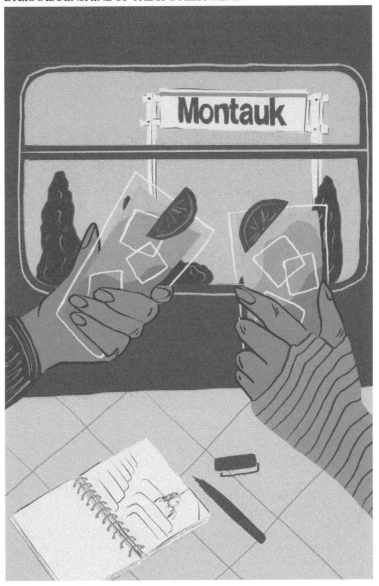

Put on your chicest black dress and largest sunglasses and whip up this homage to the bee's knees of all romantic films. It's the perfect drink for many occasions, from a swinging party in a New York apartment, to when you suddenly feel the need to sing something wistful on a fire escape.

# Bee's Knees at Tiffany's

## INGREDIENTS

| | | |
|---|---|---|
| 60ML GIN | 20ML LEMON JUICE | 20ML HONEY SYRUP (3 PARTS HONEY TO 1 PART WATER) |

Add the ingredients into an ice-filled cocktail shaker. Shake and strain into a chilled coupe. Evening gloves optional.

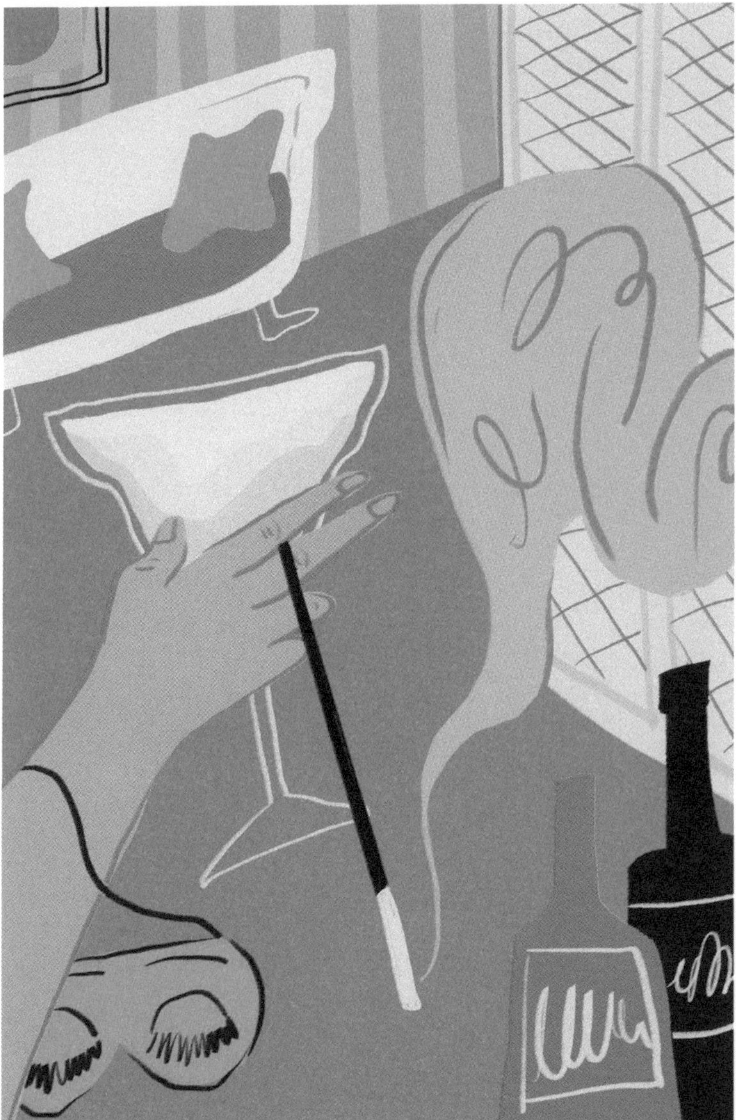

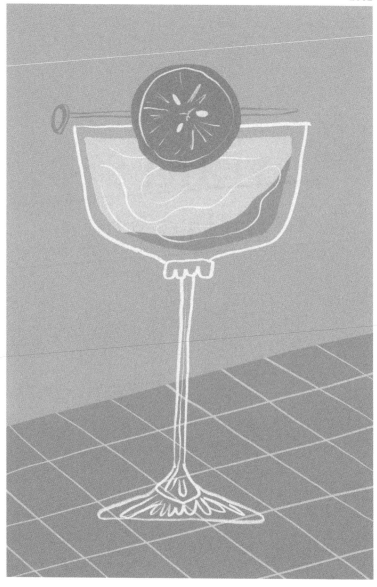

If the glamour of downtown Manhattan seems a world away, this film _and_ this cocktail may be just what you need to remind you that all it takes is a fancy coat and some J Lo-level sass to change your life. If you're paying attention, you'll realise this is actually a 'maid' style cocktail and not a Manhattan. Plot twist!

# Maid's Manhattan

## INGREDIENTS

1 DASH ABSINTHE

4 SLICES CUCUMBER

A SPRIG OF MINT

15ML SUGAR SYRUP (SEE PAGE 9)

30ML LIME JUICE

60ML WHITE RUM

50ML SODA WATER

Add the dash of the absinthe to an ice-filled cocktail glass. Top with cold tap water and leave to stand. Put three of the cucumber slices, mint, sugar syrup and lime juice into a shaker and stir gently to bruise the mint. Then add rum and ice and shake. Empty the cocktail glass and then double-strain the mix from the shaker into the cocktail glass. Top up with soda water to taste, and garnish with the last slice of cucumber.

We've all been tempted to put that shiny, lovely new thing on the credit card, but as Rebecca Bloomwood is here to show us, the pursuit of material items can only get us so far. So, instead of logging into ASOS, why not don your best green scarf, mix up this cocktail, and enjoy some vicarious shopping with Isla Fisher instead.

# DITSY BRITZY SPRITZ

## INGREDIENTS

| | | |
|---|---|---|
| 35ML KAMM & SONS | 50ML SPARKLING WHITE WINE | GRAPEFRUIT |
| 15ML ELDERFLOWER CORDIAL | 50ML SODA WATER | |

Pour all the ingredients in a glass filled with ice cubes, and stir well. Squeeze a wedge of grapefruit into the cocktail and garnish with a fresh wedge of grapefruit.

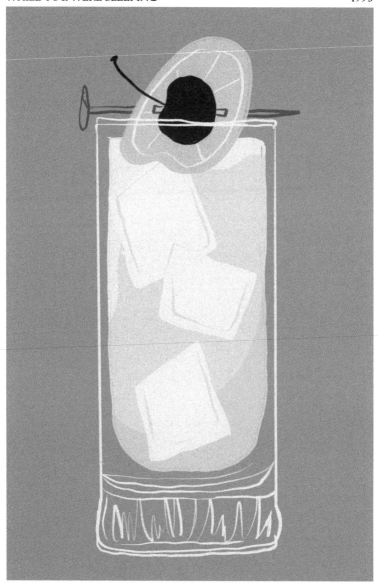

While probably not many of us have been in a situation where we have saved someone's life and then fallen for their brother, it can prove all-too-easy to get unexpectedly entangled in a misunderstanding, and not know how to get out of it. So, let's keep things simple here at least, with this sweet-and-sour gin tipple. Don't stay in the booth, Lucy!

# Chicago Collins

## INGREDIENTS

50ML GIN
25ML LEMON JUICE

20ML SUGAR SYRUP (SEE PAGE 9)
SODA WATER

LEMON OR MARASCHINO
CHERRY, TO GARNISH

Fill a tall tumbler glass with ice. Add the gin, lemon juice and sugar syrup. Top with soda water, add more ice, if necessary, to fill the glass, and stir to mix. Garnish with a lemon wedge or a Maraschino cherry.

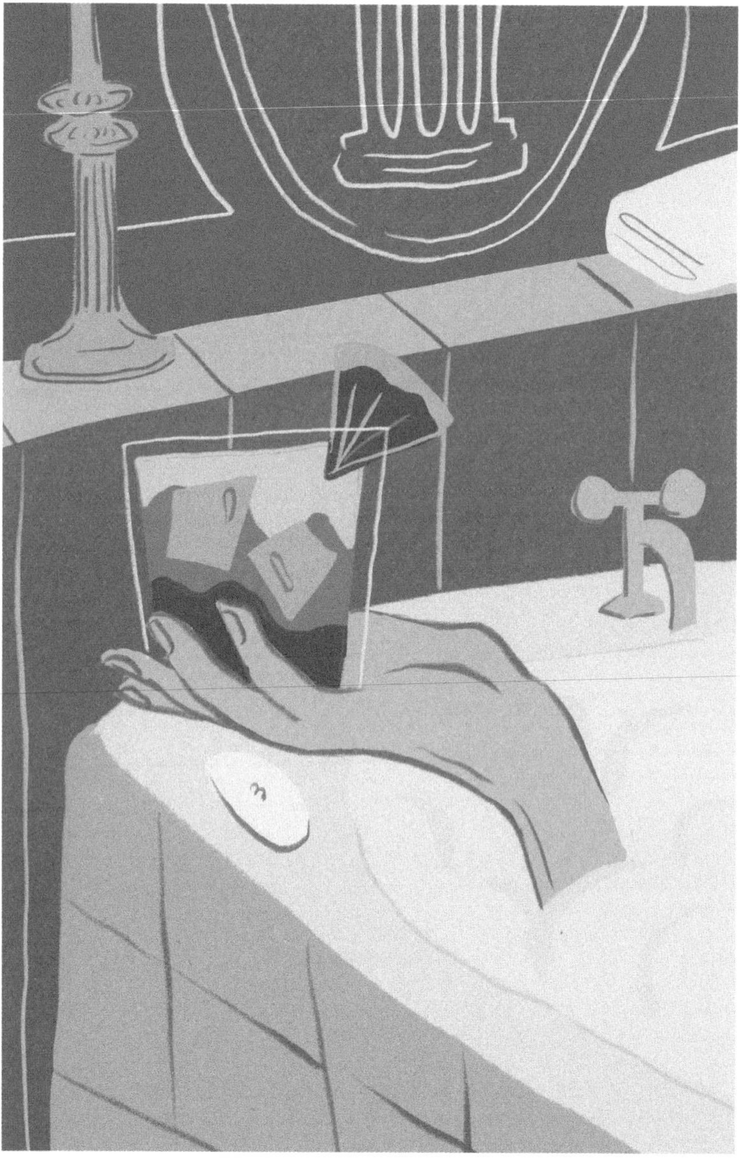

If you've never had this cocktail before, imagine a margarita got all dressed up to take a private jet to the opera. It's better than a shopping trip on Rodeo Drive and could even cheer up a sad millionaire. In fact, it's so good, you might pee your pants.

# PALOMA WOMAN

## INGREDIENTS

| | | |
|---|---|---|
| FINE SALT | 20ML LIME JUICE | 60ML PINK GRAPEFRUIT JUICE |
| 60ML TEQUILA | 10ML AGAVE SYRUP | LIME AND GRAPEFRUIT, TO GARNISH |

Put a tablespoon or so of fine salt on a plate. Rub a lime wedge around the edge of a highball glass and, turning the glass upside-down and pressing it into the plate, coat the rim of the glass with the salt. Put the tequila, lime juice, agave syrup and pink grapefruit juice in a cocktail shaker. Add ice, shake and strain into the glass, over ice, if you like your drinks as cool as Vivian's thigh-high boots. Garnish with a wedge of grapefruit.

In one version of this story, you don't try this cocktail. You carry on as you were before, missing all the signs that are right in front of you, and your life stays the way it was. But is that the version of the story you want? No, so grab your cocktail shaker, and put on the film that showed us what a break-up haircut is supposed to look like.

# SLIDING SLING

## INGREDIENTS

| | | |
|---|---|---|
| 30ML GIN | 15ML HEERING CHERRY LIQUEUR | 1 DASH ANGOSTURA BITTERS |
| 10ML COINTREAU | 15ML LIME JUICE | 120ML PINEAPPLE JUICE |
| 10ML BENEDICTINE | 10ML GRENADINE | FRUIT, TO GARNISH |

Add all the ingredients to a cocktail shaker with ice. Shake, and strain into a tall tumbler over ice. Serve with a fruit slice (orange, lemon and pineapple all work well) and something like a Maraschino cherry or raspberry.

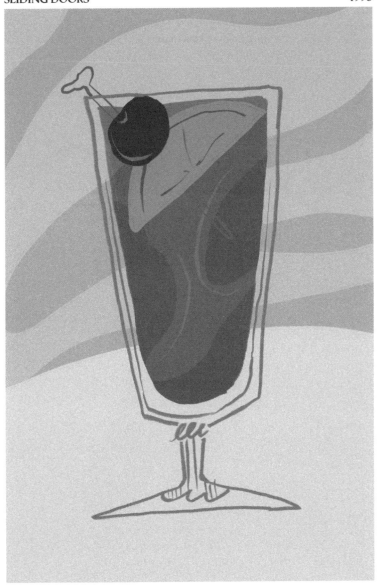

Whether it's Paris fashion week or just a regular Friday night, you'll want to put together your most stylish outfit for this one. It's the perfect drink with which to impress the boss – or anyone really. This cocktail is even cooler than Meryl Streep's icy stare.

# EL DESIGNER DIABLO

## INGREDIENTS

50ML TEQUILA

25ML CRÈME DE CASSIS

25ML LIME JUICE

GINGER ALE

LIME WEDGE

Add the first three ingredients to a tall tumbler glass filled with ice and mix. Top with ginger ale and garnish with a lime wedge.

You might not have guessed it, but rum, brandy and citrus make for the perfect cocktail mix tape. If you've been jumping from drink to drink, struggling to commit, then take this opportunity to put on a record and find out if this is the cocktail you have been waiting for...

# HIGH(BALL) FIDELITY

## INGREDIENTS

| | | |
|---|---|---|
| 50ML WHITE RUM | 50ML ORANGE JUICE | 20ML ORGEAT SYRUP |
| 20ML BRANDY OR COGNAC | 30ML LEMON JUICE | ORANGE, TO GARNISH |

Add all the ingredients to a cocktail shaker, with some ice, and shake well, before straining into an ice-filled highball glass. Garnish with a slice of orange. If you have some music-loving friends coming over, this also works well as a punch, ideally served from a suitably vintage punchbowl. Scale up the ingredients accordingly, and, if you can, chill with a big single ice cube to avoid diluting the drink too much (fill a suitable container with water and freeze overnight).

Sure, there's a whole world of glitzy, complicated cocktails out there and nothing from stopping you from trying every one. But what if the right cocktail for you is something simpler, something that's maybe been there all along? When you're ready to come home to a good, honest drink that truly understands you, you'll know where to find this martini. Just don't eat the napkin.

# ALWAYS BE MY MARTINI

## INGREDIENTS

| 10ML DRY VERMOUTH | 60ML GIN | OLIVES, TO GARNISH |

Fill a mixing glass (ideally one that's been in the fridge, as you want this drink as cold as possible) with ice, add the vermouth and stir to coat the ice. If you like your martini dry, strain out some of the vermouth and discard it. Add the gin and stir until chilled and diluted – this takes the edge of the punchiness of the neat gin. Strain into a chilled martini glass and garnish with olives.

# TIPPLES
# TO SAY
# I DO TO

Talking of doing things over and over, why does Katherine Heigl keep falling for cynical men who don't believe in marriage? Whether you love being a bridesmaid, or would rather shirk the responsibility and get seated at the 'naughty table' with all the other people the bride and groom don't trust to behave, this is the perfect drink to round off a day of celebrating someone else's (hopefully) happy-ever-after.

# Choose Me Negroni

## INGREDIENTS

| | | |
|---|---|---|
| 30ML GIN | 30ML SWEET VERMOUTH | ORANGE, TO GARNISH |
| 30ML CAMPARI | | |

Add all the alcohol to an ice-filled rocks glass, and stir (one or two large ice cubes are much better than a load of small ones here). Garnish with an orange slice or twist.

Just because everyone else is doing it, doesn't mean you have to as well. Take your time, and only have an alcoholic drink when you want one, not because you are being pressured into it. If you listen to other people, you'll end up with all the wrong cocktails. There's no shame in going virgin.

# THE 40-YEAR-OLD VIRGIN MARGARITA

## INGREDIENTS

| | | |
|---|---|---|
| FINE SALT | 30ML LIME JUICE | LIME, TO GARNISH |
| 50ML NON-ALCOHOLIC TEQUILA | 30ML ORANGE JUICE | |

To salt the rim of the margarita glass, run a wedge of lime around it, and then touch it to a plate covered with fine salt. Add all the ingredients to a shaker with ice, and carefully strain into the glass. Garnish with a lime wheel or wedge on the side of the glass.

It's a truth universally acknowledged in the romcom world, that weddings can make us do crazy things. Sure, maybe you've never hired an escort in a mistaken attempt to save face, but there's bound to have been something and, whatever it was, hopefully you had your very own TJ – the queen of all movie best friends – to bail you out.

# NICK'S MARTINI

## INGREDIENTS

| | | |
|---|---|---|
| 60ML NAVY-STRENGTH GIN | 20ML DRY VERMOUTH | CITRUS WEDGE OR ZEST TWIST OF YOUR CHOOSING |

Add the ingredients to a mixing glass filled with ice. Stir until well chilled and diluted. Strain into a martini glass or champagne coupe. Garnish with a citrus wedge or zest twist – whichever you think matches best to your style of gin.

Being unexpectedly serenaded on a crowded aeroplane may not be for everyone, but this cocktail is a guaranteed crowd-pleaser. Whether you're planning a wedding or a fun night in curled up with a romcom, pop the prosecco and pour yourself a drink that's as heartwarming as Julia and Robbie themselves. (Van Halen t-shirt optional.)

# THE WEDDING SPRITZ

## INGREDIENTS

| | | |
|---|---|---|
| 75ML PROSECCO | 25ML SODA WATER | ORANGE SLICE OR ORANGE, |
| 50ML APEROL | | TO GARNISH |

Add all the ingredients into a large wine glass filled with ice.
Gently stir and garnish with orange slices.

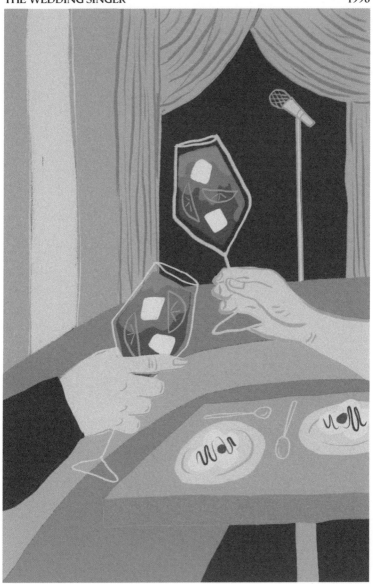

# ROMCOM QUEENS

## HOLLYWOOD'S HIGHEST-GROSSING ROMCOM ACTRESSES

**1**
## JULIA ROBERTS

**2**
## JENNIFER ANISTON

**3**
## DREW BARRYMORE

(SOURCE: THE NUMBERS)

Everyone wants the perfect wedding, but as Kate Hudson and Anne Hathaway are here to show us, there's really no need to rugby tackle your best friend to the floor as she walks down the aisle. Instead, take the heat out of the preparations for the big day with a lovely, chilled, romcom cocktail.

# A Cosmopolitan Feud

## INGREDIENTS

30ML VODKA

15ML TRIPLE SEC

15ML LIME JUICE

30ML CRANBERRY JUICE

ORANGE, TO GARNISH

Put all the ingredients into a cocktail shaker, with some ice. Shake well and strain into a chilled martini glass. Garnish with a twist of orange zest.

I do solemnly declare, that I know of no lawful impediment, why raspberry and Chambord should not be joined together with vodka, in this fun and flirty take on a martini. Whether you're off to a posh wedding or not, you won't want to miss a great opportunity to try it. Note: it may taste better if drunk while wearing a giant, early nineties, hat.

# Four Weddings and a French Martini

## INGREDIENTS

50ML VODKA

15ML CHAMBORD LIQUEUR

50ML PINEAPPLE JUICE

RASPBERRY, TO GARNISH

Add the vodka, Chambord and pineapple juice to a cocktail shaker, along with some ice. Shake and strain into a chilled martini glass. Garnish with a raspberry, and drink while putting on your best English plummy accent.

Put whoever you want on a pedestal, but make you sure you put this drink in your hand! As George would probably say, there might not be a wedding to go to, there might not even be dancing, but by god, this is a great cocktail to help you celebrate any moment you choose!

# A Champagne Toast

## INGREDIENTS

25ML VODKA

15ML ELDERFLOWER LIQUEUR OR CORDIAL

CHAMPAGNE (AROUND 75ML)

Add the vodka and elderflower liqueur to a cocktail shaker. Shake well and strain into a champagne flute or coupe, then top up with Champagne.

It's hard to get it right if you don't know what you truly want, Julia Roberts is here to teach us. Which is great advice, but less of an issue with this cocktail, which is so easy, you won't need a dress rehearsal. Like the film, the Bramble is a modern invention with something of the enduring classic about it – and it might just get to you too...

# BRIDE'S BRAMBLE

## INGREDIENTS

| | | |
|---|---|---|
| 60ML GIN | 15ML SUGAR SYRUP (SEE PAGE 9) | BLACKBERRIES, TO GARNISH |
| 30ML LEMON JUICE | 15ML CRÈME DE MÛRE LIQUEUR | |

Shake the gin, lemon juice and sugar syrup together in a cocktail shaker. Strain into a short tumbler filled with ice. Stir. Gently add some ice cubes so that the glass is full. Trickle the crème de mûre over the top and garnish with fresh blackberries.

This high-octane cocktail may appear, at first glance, to be nothing more than a regular suburban pink martini, but it's simply playing a part. The concealed weapon here – rather than a career as an assassin carefully hidden from your spouse – is a single shot of absinthe. Underestimate it at your peril.

# CONCEALED WEAPONS

## INGREDIENTS

| | | |
|---|---|---|
| 25ML ABSINTHE | 15ML SUGAR SYRUP (SEE PAGE 9) | ½ EGG WHITE (OR 1 TBSP WHIPPED AQUAFABA) |
| 25ML CHAMBORD LIQUEUR | 1 DASH ANGOSTURA BITTERS | LEMON, TO GARNISH |
| 20ML LEMON JUICE | 1 DASH PEYCHAUD'S BITTERS | |

Add all the ingredients to a cocktail shaker. Shake without ice, then add ice and shake again (wet shake). Strain into a chilled martini glass or champagne coupe. Garnish with a slice of lemon zest.

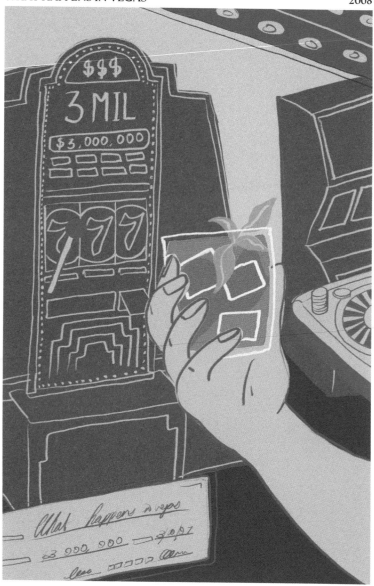

Even if you've never been fired by your dad, or dumped at the party you threw for your boyfriend, everyone's had a bad day and taken their mind off it with a weekend of partying, right? This pink cocktail is perfect if you don't want to go full 'lost weekend in Vegas'. It's fun, flirty and easy to drink – but don't forget, that doesn't mean there won't be consequences...

# LET'S GET SMASHED

## INGREDIENTS

| | | |
|---|---|---|
| 5–6 BERRIES (RASPBERRIES WORK BEST) | 6–8 MINT LEAVES 50ML BOURBON | 25ML LIME JUICE 20ML SUGAR SYRUP (SEE PAGE 9) |

Gently muddle the raspberries and mint in the bottom of a cocktail shaker, though go easy as too much smashing it up will bring out bitter flavours from the mint leaves. Add the bourbon, lime juice and sugar syrup, along with ice. Shake and strain into an ice-filled tumbler. Garnish with a lime wedge or a mint sprig (or both!).

It's wedding season! And you don't have to go to absurd lengths to crash this party. Whether you are as cynical as John and Jeremy, or you believe in everlasting love, this is the perfect drink with which to toast a summer of fancy frocks, terrible best man speeches, and that unavoidable feeling of your best pair of heels sinking into a soft lawn.

# LADY IN A WHITE DRESS

## INGREDIENTS

| | | |
|---|---|---|
| 50ML GIN | 20M TRIPLE SEC | LEMON, TO GARNISH |
| 20ML LEMON JUICE | EGG WHITE (OR 2 TBSP WHIPPED AQUAFABA), OPTIONAL | |

Add all the ingredients to a cocktail shaker. Shake without ice, then add ice and shake again. Strain into a chilled goblet glass or champagne coupe. Garnish with a strip of lemon peel, and rush to catch the bouquet.

# WINTER HEART-WARMERS

If a more dashing drink comes along to try to turn your head, don't be fooled by its easy charm. A dark 'n' stormy may be brooding, a little reserved and hard to get to know, but this is a cocktail that likes you just the way you are.

# Bridget's Dark 'n' Stormy

## INGREDIENTS

| 50ML DARK RUM | 15ML LIME JUICE | 150ML GINGER BEER |
| --- | --- | --- |

Fill a highball glass with ice. Pour in the rum and lime juice, then top with ginger beer to taste – use less if you prefer things a little stronger and more intense...

Have you ever wondered if you are... destined to drink this cocktail? Whether you think your choice of drink should be decided by the whims of fate, the vagaries of chance, or simply what happens to be in your booze cupboard, at least remain open to the possibility of a life-changing encounter with this drink.

# WHAT'S YOUR NAME?

### INGREDIENTS

25ML BOURBON
25ML GREENGAGE LIQUEUR
15ML LEMON JUICE

10ML AGAVE SYRUP
50ML GINGER ALE

A SPLASH OF LAGER
LEMON, TO GARNISH

Add the bourbon, greengage liqueur, lemon juice and agave syrup to a cocktail shaker. Add ice and shake well. Strain into a goblet glass filled with ice. Top with the ginger ale and lager. Garnish with a single glove and twist of lemon zest.

As we know from many romcoms – and particularly this one – timing is everything, opportunities are easy to miss, and misunderstandings can get in the way. So don't let the chance to try this sweet, but grown-up, cocktail slip through your fingers. Yes, boy–girl friendships can be complicated, but fortunately, this cocktail is very simple.

# LOVE FROM HARVARD

### INGREDIENTS

| | | |
|---|---|---|
| 60ML COGNAC | 2–3 DASHES ANGOSTURA BITTERS | ORANGE, TO GARNISH |
| 20ML SWEET VERMOUTH | SODA WATER | |

Fill a mixing glass with ice. Add the cognac, sweet vermouth and bitters and stir until chilled. Strain into a tall goblet, then top it up with around 50ml (a double shot) of soda water. Garnish with a wedge of orange.

Sure, it's easy to be cynical. Maybe you want to write off this cocktail as a self-regarding drink that thinks a little too much of itself (why is there *egg?!*), but take some time away from the daily grind to get to know it, and just see what happens. Maybe Ryan Reynolds appearing in a helicopter or – more fun – rapping with Betty White in the woods.

# THE NEW YORK SOUR

## INGREDIENTS

50ML WHISKEY, BOURBON OR RYE
25ML LEMON JUICE
15ML (1 TBSP) SUGAR SYRUP
(SEE PAGE 9)

1 EGG WHITE (OR 2 TBSP OF
WHIPPED AQUAFABA)
2–3 DASHES ANGOSTURA BITTERS

15ML FULL-BODIED RED WINE
LEMON, TO GARNISH

Add the whiskey, lemon juice, sugar syrup and egg white/aquafaba to a cocktail shaker. Shake without ice, then add ice and shake again. Strain into a rocks glass over ice and add the bitters. Then gently pour the red wine over the top, and garnish with lemon wedge.

You could make this once, you could make it every day – that's up to you! It's a tiny bit sour at the start, but it becomes sweet at the end, and that's what we want from a romcom cocktail. This is the drink to remind you to always live in the moment. Plus, Punxsutawney Phil predicts that you will love it.

# Greyhound Day

## INGREDIENTS

50ML VODKA OR GIN (IT WORKS WITH EITHER!)

50ML PINK GRAPEFRUIT JUICE

5ML SUGAR SYRUP (SEE PAGE 9)

GRAPEFRUIT SLICE, TO GARNISH

Add the vodka/gin, grapefruit juice and sugar syrup into an ice-filled cocktail shaker. Shake and strain into a tumbler filled with ice. Pop that grapefruit slice on the side and play the Pennsylvania Polka.

If someone offers you an LA mansion or a quaint cottage in which to spend Christmas, you'd be mad to say no. If neither are forthcoming, however, a classic snowball should get you in the mood for a little festive romance. So rummage in the cupboard for the Advocaat and prepare to obsess over 'cottagecore'. If you want to put a hankie on your face, that's entirely up to you.

# HOUSESWAP SNOWBALL

## INGREDIENTS

10ML LIME JUICE
50ML ADVOCAAT

100ML FIZZY LEMONADE

1 MARASCHINO CHERRY, TO GARNISH

Fill a large bowl glass with ice. Add the lime juice followed by the Advocaat. Pour over the lemonade and stir gently. Garnish with a Maraschino cherry.

On Wednesdays, we drink a Mean Martini. Or on any day, actually, because there are no stupid rules and Plastic cliques in this cocktail hour. So, don't worry about who's dating who, or if anyone is gossiping behind your back. Get your real friends together, and try this sweet and surprising twist on a martini. Just watch out for that bin, there.

138

### INGREDIENTS

| | | |
|---|---|---|
| 50ML GIN | 15ML LEMON JUICE | ORANGE, TO GARNISH |
| 15ML COINTREAU | 1 TSP ORANGE MARMALADE | |

Add all the ingredients to a cocktail shaker. Shake hard over ice and double strain into a chilled martini glass or champagne coupe. Garnish with a slice of orange.

It might seem crazy, or far-fetched, or like it wouldn't work. But sometimes, you just have to believe that you could mix wine, brandy and fruit, and destiny will take care of the rest. Just like this Nora Ephron classic, in which the meet-cute happens at the end, rather than the beginning of the film, this is a drink that breaks so many of the rules, but that makes us love it all the more.

# SLEEPLESS IN SANGRIA

## INGREDIENTS (SERVES 6)

750ML BOTTLE RIOJA (OR OTHER LIGHT RED SPANISH WINE).

100ML BRANDY

2 ORANGES, CHOPPED

JUICE OF A LEMON

1 LEMON, CHOPPED

750ML BOTTLE RIOJA (OR OTHER LIGHT RED SPANISH WINE).

100ML BRANDY

450G MIXED FRUIT (STRAWBERRIES, KIWIS, APPLES... WHATEVER YOU LIKE, REALLY)

4 TBSP CASTER SUGAR

350ML SPARKLING WATER

In a jug, muddle the chopped oranges, lemon juice and chopped lemon and stir in the sugar. Then, pour in the rioja and brandy, stir, then refrigerate for at least two hours. Once refrigerated, mix in the remaining ingredients and serve in large wine glasses or tumblers. Ideally at the top of the Empire State Building, but if this isn't an option, almost anywhere else will do.

# TOP 3
# MEG RYAN
# ROMCOMS

## 1
## *SLEEPLESS IN SEATTLE*
### (1993)

## 2
## *YOU'VE GOT MAIL*
### (1998)

## 3
## *WHEN HARRY MET SALLY*
### (1989)

Why are people in romcoms always going on dates to the opera? Next time the moon is full, why not try this tangy, gingery drink. You could listen to *La Boheme* – though it would probably feel less dramatic than Cher's incredible hair in this film. (And yes, if you have always wondered, Nicolas Cage really was missing a tooth when he played Ronny.)

# (MOSCOW) MULE-STRUCK

## INGREDIENTS

50ML VODKA
HALF A LIME, JUICED

GINGER BEER

SLICE OF LIME, AND A MINT SPRIG, TO GARNISH

Add the vodka and lime juice to a highball glass or small punch cup and stir. Fill with ice and top with ginger beer. You can add Angostura bitters, if you like an extra herby kick. Add a slice of lime and a sprig of mint, to garnish.

Travel back to the heady days of the late nineties, when the idea of two strangers meeting via the internet seemed kind-of crazy. This is a grown-up cocktail that pairs perfectly with the smell of bookstores and a business rivalry with romantic potential...

# YOU'VE GOT RUSTY NAIL

## INGREDIENTS

50ML SCOTCH WHISKY          1 TBSP DRAMBUIE          LEMON, TO GARNISH

Pour the scotch whisky and Drambuie into a short tumbler filled with ice and stir gently to combine. Garnish with a slice of lemon and a copy of Jane Austen's *Pride and Prejudice* on the side.

Nothing says Christmas like Andrew Lincoln confessing his love to his best friend's wife, Colin Firth proposing to someone he's never had a conversation with, or Alan Rickman disappointing Emma Thompson. Like some of the plot strands of *Love Actually*, an alcoholic drink made from egg, rum and milk might seem a bit wrong, but it's all very sweet, perfectly Christmassy, and everything works out in the end.

# EGGNOG ACTUALLY

## INGREDIENTS (SERVES 10)

| | | |
|---|---|---|
| 100G CASTER SUGAR | 150ML DARK RUM | WHOLE NUTMEG |
| 12 EGGS | 1 LITRE DOUBLE CREAM | CINNAMON STICK, TO GARNISH |
| 350ML COGNAC | 1 LITRE FULL-FAT MILK | |

This takes a little longer to make than most of the cocktails here, so it's best to make a batch for all the visitors who have heard you are watching *Love Actually* and want to pop round. Take a large mixing bowl or punchbowl. Whisk the sugar into the eggs, then beat in the cognac and rum. Add the cream and beat again. Add the milk and beat a final time. Ladle into ice-filled eggnog glasses and garnish each with a light sprinkle of freshly grated nutmeg. Add cinnamon sticks for an extra Christmassy flourish.

# ROMCOM CHECKLIST

Consider yourself a romcom connoisseur? Use this list of
the greatest romcoms of all time to keep track of how
many you've seen, and how many cocktails you've drunk.

| FILM | COCKTAIL |
|---|---|
| ☐ Roman Holiday (1953) | ☐ Ro-Manhattan Holiday (p.66) |
| ☐ Breakfast at Tiffany's (1961) | ☐ Bee's Knees at Tiffany's (p.80) |
| ☐ Splash (1984) | ☐ Tom Hanky Panky (p.44) |
| ☐ Moonstruck (1987) | ☐ (Moscow) Mule-struck (p.144) |
| ☐ When Harry Met Sally (1989) | ☐ When Harry Met Daiquiri (p.14) |
| ☐ Pretty Woman (1990) | ☐ Paloma Woman (p.88) |
| ☐ Groundhog Day (1993) | ☐ Greyhound Day (p.134) |
| ☐ Sleepless in Seattle (1993) | ☐ Sleepless in Sangria (p.140) |
| ☐ Four Weddings and a Funeral (1994) | ☐ Four Weddings and a French Martini (p.112) |
| ☐ Clueless (1995) | ☐ Clueless Colada (p.16) |
| ☐ While You Were Sleeping (1995) | ☐ Chicago Collins (p.86) |

| FILM | COCKTAIL |
|------|----------|
| ☐ Picture Perfect (1997) | ☐ Boston Bound (p.76) |
| ☐ My Best Friend's Wedding (1997) | ☐ A Champagne Toast (p.114) |
| ☐ There's Something About Mary (1998) | ☐ There's Something About (Bloody) Mary (p.52) |
| ☐ How Stella Got Her Groove Back (1998) | ☐ Stella's Ginger Brew (p.62) |
| ☐ Sliding Doors (1998) | ☐ Sliding Sling (p.90) |
| ☐ The Wedding Singer (1998) | ☐ The Wedding Spritz (p.106) |
| ☐ You've Got Mail (1998) | ☐ You've Got Rusty Nail (p.146) |
| ☐ 10 Things I Hate About You (1999) | ☐ 10 Things I Hate About Woo Woo (p.22) |
| ☐ Never Been Kissed (1999) | ☐ Josie's Julep (p.38) |
| ☐ Notting Hill (1999) | ☐ Notting Bellini (p.70) |
| ☐ Runaway Bride (1999) | ☐ Bride's Bramble (p.116) |
| ☐ High Fidelity (2000) | ☐ High(ball) Fidelity (p.94) |
| ☐ What Happens in Vegas (2008) | ☐ Let's Get Smashed (p.120) |
| ☐ Legally Blonde (2001) | ☐ Elle Sorority Presidente (p.36) |
| ☐ America's Sweethearts (2001) | ☐ Americano Sweethearts (p.74) |
| ☐ Bridget Jones' Diary (2001) | ☐ Bridget's Dark 'n' Stormy (p.126) |

151

| FILM | COCKTAIL |
|------|----------|
| ☐ Serendipity (2001) | ☐ What's Your Name? (p.128) |
| ☐ Sweet Home Alabama (2002) | ☐ Sweet Home Alabama Slammer (p.50) |
| ☐ Maid in Manhattan (2002) | ☐ Maid's Manhattan (p.82) |
| ☐ How to Lose a Guy in 10 Days (2003) | ☐ How to Lose a Gimlet in 10 Days (p.18) |
| ☐ Love Actually (2003) | ☐ Eggnog Actually (p.148) |
| ☐ 13 Going on 30 (2004) | ☐ Matty-dor (p.32) |
| ☐ 50 First Dates (2004) | ☐ Oopsy (Brandy) Daisy (p.58) |
| ☐ Eternal Sunshine of the Spotless Mind (2004) | ☐ Eternal Tequila Sunrise of the Spotless Mind (p.78) |
| ☐ Mean Girls (2004) | ☐ Mean Martini (p.138) |
| ☐ Just Like Heaven (2005) | ☐ The Tenant Reviver (p.24) |
| ☐ The 40-Year-Old Virgin (2005) | ☐ The 40-Year-Old Virgin Margarita (p.102) |
| ☐ The Wedding Date (2005) | ☐ Nick's Martini (p.104) |
| ☐ Mr and Mrs Smith (2005) | ☐ Concealed Weapons (p.118) |
| ☐ Wedding Crashers (2005) | ☐ Lady in a White Dress (p.122) |
| ☐ Failure to Launch (2006) | ☐ Tripp Sour (p.34) |
| ☐ The Devil Wears Prada (2006) | ☐ El Designer Diablo (p.92) |

| FILM | COCKTAIL |
|---|---|
| ☐ The Holiday (2006) | ☐ Houseswap Snowball (p.136) |
| ☐ Forgetting Sarah Marshall (2008) | ☐ Forgetting Sarah Mai Tai (p.42) |
| ☐ Mamma Mia (2008) | ☐ Mamma Cuba Libre (p.56) |
| ☐ 27 Dresses (2008) | ☐ Choose Me Negroni (p.100) |
| ☐ The Ugly Truth (2009) | ☐ Morning Show Fizz (p.28) |
| ☐ 500 days of Summer (2009) | ☐ 500 Flavours of Mojito (p.48) |
| ☐ He's Just Not That Into You (2009) | ☐ He's Just Not That Into Sex on the Beach (p.60) |
| ☐ Confessions of a Shopaholic (2009) | ☐ Ditsy Britzy Spritz (p.84) |
| ☐ Bride Wars (2009) | ☐ A Cosmopolitan Feud (p.110) |
| ☐ The Proposal (2009) | ☐ The New York Sour (p.132) |
| ☐ Easy A (2010) | ☐ Easy (A)mbrosia (p.26) |
| ☐ Flipped (2010) | ☐ Rum Flipped (p.64) |
| ☐ Crazy Stupid Love (2011) | ☐ Crazy Shandy Love (p.20) |
| ☐ No Strings Attached (2011) | ☐ No Strings Between the Sheets (p.30) |
| ☐ About Time (2013) | ☐ Back in Time (p.54) |
| ☐ Love, Rosie (2014) | ☐ Love from Harvard (p.130) |
| ☐ Always Be My Maybe (2019) | ☐ Always Be My Martini (p.96) |

153

# INDEX

156

# CREDITS

**I'LL HAVE WHAT SHE'S HAVING (pp 12-39)** *When Harry Met Sally* (1989) directed by Rob Reiner, produced by Rob Reiner, Andrew Scheinman. *Clueless* (1995) directed by Amy Heckerling, produced by Scott Rudin, Robert Lawrence. *How to Lose a Guy in 10 Days* (2003) directed by Donald Petrie, produced by Lynda Obst, Robert Evans. *Crazy Stupid Love* (2011) directed by Glenn Ficarra and John Requa, produced by Eryn Brown, Steve Carell, Vance DeGeneres, Denise Di Novi, Jeffrey Harlacker, Charlie Hartsock and David Siegel. *10 Things I Hate About You* (1999) directed by Gil Junger, produced by Jeffrey Chernov, Jody Hedien, Andrew Lazar, Seth Jaret, Greg Silverman. *Just Like Heaven* (2005) directed by Mark Waters, produced by Laurie MacDonald, Walter F. Parkes, Marc Levy. *Easy A* (2010) directed by Will Gluck, produced by Zanne Devine, Will Gluck. *The Ugly Truth* (2009) directed by Robert Luketic, produced by Gary Lucchesi, Tom Rosenberg. *No Strings Attached* (2011) directed by Ivan Reitman, produced by Ivan Reitman, Joe Medjuck, Jeffrey Clifford. *13 Going on 30* (2004) directed by Gary Winick, produced by Susan Arnold, Gina Matthews, Donna Arkoff Roth. *Failure to Launch* (2006) directed by Tom Dey, produced by Scott Aversano, Ron Bozman, Karen Dexter and Scott Rudin. *Legally Blonde* (2001) directed by Robert Luketic, produced by Marc E. Platt, Ric Kidney. *Never Been Kissed* (1999) directed by Raja Gosnell, produced by Drew Barrymore, Jeffrey Downer, Sandy Isaac, Nancy Juvonen. **SUMMER OF LOVE (pp 40-67)** *Forgetting Sarah Marshall* (2008) directed by Nicholas Stoller, produced by Judd Apatow, Shauna Robertson. *Splash* (1984) directed by Ron Howard, produced by Brian Grazer, Ron Howard. *Flipped* (2010), directed by Rob Reiner, produced by Rob Reiner, Alan Greisman. *500 Days of Summer* (2009) directed by Marc Webb, produced by Mason Novick, Jessica Tuchinsky. *Sweet Home Alabama* (2002) directed by Andy Tennant, produced by Neal H. Moritz, Stokely Chaffin. *About Time* (2013) directed by Richard Curtis, produced by Tim Bevan, Eric Fellner. *There's Something About Mary* (1998) directed by Peter Farrelly, Bobby Farrelly, produced by Frank Beddor, Michael Steinberg. *Mamma Mia* (2008) directed by Phyllida Lloyd, produced by Judy Craymer, Gary Goetzman. *50 First Dates* (2004) directed by Peter Segal, produced by Jack Giarraputo, Steve Golin, Nancy Juvonen. *He's Just Not That Into You* (2009) directed by Ken Kwapis, produced by Nancy Juvonen, Drew Barrymore. *How Stella Got Her Groove Back* (1998) directed by Kevin Rodney Sullivan, produced by Deborah Schindler. *Roman Holiday* (1953) directed by William Wyler, produced by William Wyler. **DOWNTOWN DRINKS (pp 68-97)** *Notting Hill* (1999) directed by Roger Michell, produced by Duncan Kenworthy. *America's Sweethearts* (2001) directed by Joe Roth, produced by Billy Crystal, Susan Arnold, Donna Arkoff Roth. *Picture Perfect* (1997) directed by Glenn Gordon Caron, produced by Erwin Stoff. *Eternal Sunshine of the Spotless Mind* (2004) directed by Michel Gondry, produced by Anthony Bregman, Steve Golin. *Breakfast at Tiffany's* (1961) directed by Blake Edwards, produced by Martin Jurow, Richard Shepherd. *Maid in Manhattan* (2002) directed by Wayne Wang, produced by Elaine Goldsmith-Thomas, Jennifer Lopez. *Confessions of a Shopaholic* (2009) directed by P.J. Hogan, produced by Jerry Bruckheimer. *While You Were Sleeping* (1995) directed by Jon Turteltaub, produced by Roger Birnbaum, Joe Roth. *Pretty Woman* (1990) directed by Garry Marshall, produced by Arnon Milchan, Steven Reuther. *Sliding Doors* (1998) directed by Peter Howitt, produced by Sydney Pollack, Philippa Braithwaite. *The Devil Wears Prada* (2006) directed by David Frankel, produced by Wendy Finerman. *High Fidelity* (2000) directed by Stephen Frears, produced by Tim Bevan, Rudd Simmons, John Cusack. *Always Be My Maybe* (2019) directed by Nahnatchka Khan, produced by Nathan Kahane, Erin Westerman. **TIPPLES TO SAY I DO TO (pp 98-123)** *27 Dresses* (2008) directed by Anne Fletcher, produced by Roger Birnbaum, Jonathan Clickman, Becki Cross Trujillo, Michael Mayer, Robert F. Newmyer, Erin Stam and Gary Barber. *The 40-Year-Old Virgin* (2005) directed by Judd Apatow, produced by Judd Apatow, Andrew Jay Cohen, Jon Poll, Shauna Robertson, Seth Rogen, Clayton Townsend. *The Wedding Date* (2005) directed by Clare Kilner, produced by Jessica Bendinger, Mairi Bett, Paul Brooks, Michelle Chydzik Sowa, Jeff Levine, Nathalie Marciano, Scott Niemeyer, Jim Reeve, Steve Robbins, Norm Waitt. *The Wedding Singer* (1998) directed by Tim Herlihy, produced by Richard Brener, Jack Giarraputo, Brad Grey, Ira Shuman, Robert Simonds, Sandy Wernick, Brian Witten. *Bride Wars* (2009) directed by Gary Winick produced by Jay Cohen, Jonathan Filley, Kate Hudson, Matt Luber, Tony Ludwig, Arnon Milchan, Alan Riche, Devon Wilson, Julie Yorn. *Four Weddings and a Funeral* (1994) directed by Mike Newell, produced by Duncan Kenworthy, Tim Bevan, Richard Curtis, Eric Fellner. *My Best Friend's Wedding* (1997) directed by P.J.Hogan, produced by Ron Bass, Gil Netter, Patricia Whitcher, Jerry Zucker. *Runaway Bride* (1999) directed by Garry Marshall, produced by Tom Rosenberg, Ted Field, Robert W. Cort, Scott Kroopf, James Murray, Kevin Sussman, Mario Iscovich, Gary Lucchesi, David Madden, Ellen H. Schwartz, Karen Stirgwolt, Ted Tannebaum, Richard S. Wright. *Mr and Mrs Smith* (2005) directed by Doug Liman, produced by Arnon Milchan, Akiva Goldsman, Lucas Foster, Patrick Wachsberger, Eric McLeod Dawn Carter Erik Feig Lucas Foster Akiva Goldsman, Kim H. Winther. *What Happens in Vegas* (2008) directed by Tom Vaughan, produced by Michael Aguilar, Joe Caracciolo Jr, Dean Georgaris,Shawn Levy, Tom McNulty, Arnon Milchan, Jimmy Miller. *Wedding Crashers* (2005) directed by David Dobkin, produced by Peter Abrams, Cale Boyter, Richard Brener, Toby Emmerich, Robert L. Levy, Andrew Panay, Guy Riedel. **WINTER HEART WARMERS (pp 124-149)** *Bridget Jones' Diary* (2001) directed by Sharon Maguire, produced by Tim Bevan, Jonathan Cavendish, Liza Chasin, Eric Fellner, Helen Fielding, Debra Hayward, Peter McAleese. *Serendipity* (2001) directed by Peter Chelsom, produced by Peter Abrams, Robbie Brenner, Simon Fields, Julie Goldstein, Amy J. Kaufman, Robert L. Levy, Bob Osher, Andrew Panay, Amy Slotnick. *Love, Rosie* (2014) directed by Christian Ditter, produced by Simon Brooks, Don Carmody, James Flynn, Robert Kulzer, Jonnie Malachi, Martin Moszkowicz, Bernhard Thür. *The Proposal* (2009) directed by Anne Fletcher, produced by David Hoberman, Todd Lieberman. *Groundhog Day* (1993) directed by Harold Ramis, produced by Trevor Albert, Harold Ramis. *The Holiday* (2006) directed by Nancy Myers, produced by Bruce A. Block, Jennifer Eatz, Suzanne Farwell, Nancy Meyers. *Mean Girls* (2004) directed by Mark Waters, produced by Lorne Michaels. *Sleepless in Seattle* (1993) directed by Nora Ephron, produced by Gary Foster, Nora Ephron. *Moonstruck* (1987) directed by Norman Jewison, produced by Norman Jewison, Bonnie Palef, Patrick J. Palmer. *You've Got Mail* (1998) directed by Nora Ephron, produced by Nora Ephron, Lauren Shuler Donner. *Love Actually* (2003) directed by Richard Curtis produced by Tim Bevan, Liza Chasin, Eric Fellner, Debra Hayward, Duncan Kenworthy, Chris Thompson.

First published in 2024 by Pop Press
an imprint of Ebury Publishing

20 Vauxhall Bridge Road,
London SW1V 2SA

Pop Press is part of the Penguin Random House
group of companies whose addresses can be
found at global.penguinrandomhouse.com

 Penguin
Random House
UK

Text © Pop Press 2024

Illustrations:
Evi-O.Studio | Katherine Zhang, Siena Zadro
Text design:
Evi-O.Studio | Katherine Zhang

www.penguin.co.uk

A CIP catalogue record for this book
is available from the British Library

ISBN 9781529936360

Printed and bound in Malaysia by Times Offset (M) Sdn Bhd

The authorised representative in the EEA
is Penguin Random House Ireland,
Morrison Chambers, 32 Nassau Street,
Dublin D02 YH68

 MIX
Paper | Supporting
responsible forestry
FSC® C018179